# The Life Guards

## DRESS AND APPOINTMENTS
## 1660-1914

**Charles Stadden**

ALMARK PUBLISHING CO., LTD., LONDON

First published — December 1971

ISBN 0 85524 048 2 (hard cover edition)
ISBN 0 85524 049 0 (paper covered edition)

Printed in Great Britain by
Martins Press Ltd., London EC1R 0EN
for the publishers, Almark Publishing Co. Ltd.,
270 Burlington Road, New Malden, Surrey, KT3 4NL.

# Foreword

IN the following pages the illustrations bring together some of the known details of the uniform of the Life Guards, from the beginnings up to the full dress uniform as worn on State duties today. It would be impossible to cover all orders of dress in this small book, but where possible both back and front views are shown and full colour descriptions are given in the text of the line drawings. In addition, eight colour plates show orders of dress at various stages in the regiment's history and supplement the drawings.

My grateful thanks to Captain R. G. Hollies-Smith, Mr. R. G. Harris, Major A. McAnnand and the Parker Gallery for their great help and advice. Also for the many contributors to the *Journal of the Society of Army Historical Research* without whose efforts this work would be impossible. The following is a bibliography of reference sources used in preparing this book:

*Journal of the Society of Army Historical Research* (49 Volumes, various issues)

*Military Drawings and Paintings in the Royal Collection* (2 Volumes) (Dawnay, Haswell Miller)

*British Military Uniforms from Contemporary Pictures* (Carman)

P. W. Reynolds—MSS.

*History of the Uniforms of the British Army* (5 Volumes) (C. C. P. Lawson)

*The Dress of the 1st Regiment of Life Guards in Three Centuries* (Broughton)

*Story of the Household Cavalry* (Sir George Arthur)

*Dress Regulations, 1822, 1834, 1846 and 1900*

*Distinction of Rank of Regimental Officers* (J.S.A.H.R.) (Dawnay)

*Household Brigade Magazine*

*Navy and Army Illustrated* (15 Volumes)

*Badges of Warrant and Non-Commissioned Rank in the British Army* (J.S.A.H.R.) (Dawnay)

MSS from Author's Collection

Collection of Mr. R. G. Harris of Southsea

## CONTENTS


| Section | Page |
|---|---|
| *Foreword* | *3* |
| *Introduction* | *5* |
| *Uniform Drawings and Photographs: Figs 1–55* | *8–65* |
| *Colour Plates: Plates 1–8* | *17, 20, 21, 24, 25, 28, 29, 32* |

Squadron Corporal-Major of the 1st Life Guards in 1896, carrying his squadron standard. Uniform is as described with Figs 54–56 in this book. Note the musketry proficiency badge on his cuff.

# Introduction

THE famous regiment now known as the Life Guards are descended from two troops of horse that were composed of gentlemen cavaliers who had followed King Charles II into exile after the Civil War.

At the Restoration these troops were known as the King's Troop and the Duke of York's Troop, and a third was added which was called The Duke of Albemarle's Troop. The establishment was 200 men to each. The third, or Duke of Albemarle's Troop, later became known as the Queen's Troop.

Between 1661 and 1689 various changes were made in the precedence of the troops and after the union with Scotland a Scots troop was added, now making four troops of *Horse Guards*. It was not until 1788, on the re-organization of the Regiment that the title became *Life Guards*. They remained at this four-troop establishment until 1746 when they were reduced to only two.

## HORSE GRENADIERS

In the meantime a troop of Horse Grenadier Guards had been formed. This took place in 1678 and these were divided into first three divisions, afterwards four, one being attached to each troop of Horse Guards. A second, or Scots Troop, of Horse Grenadier Guards was later added. The Horse Grenadier Guards were recruited in the same way as the Line Cavalry and were not of the same standing as the Private Gentlemen of the Horse Guards. In 1746, when the four troops of Horse Guards were reduced to two, the 1st and 2nd Troops of Horse Grenadier Guards were attached to each.

The year 1788 marked the re-organization into two regiments, the 1st Troop of Horse Guards and 1st Troop of Horse Grenadier Guards becoming the 1st Regiment of Life Guards, while the 2nd Troop or Queen's Troop of Horse Guards and the 2nd or Scots Troop of Horse Grenadier Guards became the 2nd Regiment of Life Guards.

## AMALGAMATION

It was not until 1922 that the Life Guards became a single Regiment as a result of the drastic defence reductions implemented at that time. The 1st and 2nd Regiments were duly amalgamated, the dress distinctions of both being retained. 'A' and 'B' Squadrons had the crimson flask cord and 'C' and 'D' the blue until 1927 when, due to further economies, the Regiment was reduced to three squadrons and the red flask cord was adopted by all ranks.

The Regiment, being the bodyguard to the Sovereign, in the early days only took the field when the King was present in person. But the Regiment saw much service during the campaigns of William III and part of the Regiment was at Dettingen with George I. The Regiment covered the retreat of the Army at Fontenoy in 1745.

In 1812 squadrons from each of the Household Cavalry Regiments were sent to the Peninsular, where they joined Wellington's Army and saw distinguished service in the campaigns of 1812–13–14. Later at Waterloo, in 1815, the 1st Cavalry Brigade, the two regiments of Life Guards and Blues commanded by Lord Edward Somerset, covered themselves with glory on that memorable day.

After Waterloo the 1st and 2nd Life Guards remained at home on various State duties and it was not until 1882 that the chance of again going on foreign service presented itself. When the Arabi rebellion began in June 1882, three squadrons of Household Cavalry joined Wolseley's force and again distinguished themselves in the subsequent fighting. At Kassassin on August 28 and at Tel-el-Kebir the Life Guards bore their full share in the fighting. In October 1882 the Life Guards returned to England.

In 1884 they again went to Egypt and took part in the Nile Expedition mounted on camels; they were engaged in battle at Abu Klea where they suffered many casualties. They were subsequently with Stewart's Column on their march across the desert from Korti to Metammeh.

The Life Guards went to France in World War I, exchanging their full dress for drab khaki and fought in the trenches along with the infantry. They were at Ypres, and in the bitter fighting at Passchendaele.

In 1939 the Household Cavalry were still a horsed regiment and took their mounts to the Middle East. They took part in the crushing of the Rashid Ali conspiracy and relief of the RAF station at Habbangah. The Regiment were at last armoured in 1941 as the 1st Household Cavalry Regiment and fought in the Middle East and Italy. The 2nd Household Cavalry Regiment headed the chase across the Seine, and took part in the battles in France and Germany till the end of the war.

Since World War II the Life Guards has seen active service in the Canal Zone, Cyprus, Aden, and the Oman States, as well as carrying out the usual State duties in London.

*The band of the 2nd Life Guards shown on parade, probably at Windsor, in 1880. They are in dismounted parade order. Note the boy cymbal player in the rear rank. Beyond the band are the regiment's Staff Officers (cocked hats) and beyond them the rest of the regiment formed up for a dismounted parade.*

*Staff Corporal Farrier of 1st Life Guards in 1896. See Fig 52 for a fuller description of the uniform. With distinctive blue tunic and axe, the farrier has always commanded attention.*

# The Uniforms

## Fig 1: Gentleman, Duke of York's Troop of Horse Guards, 1661

*The engravings by Wencelaus Hollar of the coronation of Charles II show the uniform of His Majesty's Horse Guards from which the detail of Fig 1 is taken. The head-dress was a high crowned buff-coloured hat with red, white and black feathers. The short scarlet coat was laced with gold, the short sleeves edged with loops of ribbon. The breeches, also decorated with ribbon and laced with gold, were of scarlet cloth. The cuirass was black for the Duke of York's Troop and a red scarf was worn round the waist. The sword was carried in a shoulder belt, evidently worn under the cuirass; the carbine belt was worn over it. Pistols in holsters and a carbine were carried as armament as well as the sword. The high boots and equipment were of a buff colour. The housings were heavily laced in gold.*

*The King's Troop of Horse Guards wore a bright polished steel cuirass over a buff coat. The hat had white and red feathers and round the waist was a red scarf. The style was otherwise exactly similar to the Duke of York's Troop shown.*

# Fig 2: Officer, 1st Troop Horse Guards, 1672 (and Private Gentleman)

*Fig 2 detail is from an oil-painting of Major-General Randolph Egerton. The head-dress is black felt with a narrow gold lacing round the brim. What may possibly be a red feather shows above the brim. The 1st Troop had red and white feathers and this could well be what is shown. Coat is scarlet with blue cuffs and gold buttons. What looks like gold thread embroidery is seen round the pocket and down the front of the coat. The sleeves are also possibly similarly embroidered. The long buff waistcoat is embroidered in gold. The boots appear to be rather low, and it may be that the tops have been turned down as was the fashion at times.*

*A natural-coloured wig rests on the shoulders, underneath which is a black cloth. The cravat has laced edges and a crimson bow to tie it. A very large crimson sash is worn over the right shoulder and tied on the left hip. The sword is worn under the coat and a slit in the coat allows the hilt to come through. The sword hilt was gilt, with black scabbard and gilt mounts. The gloves appear to be of a natural leather colour.*

*No saddlecloth shows, but the holster caps are of crimson cloth embroidered in gold, though the fine detail is not clear. The horse furniture is black leather with crimson ribbons on the brow-band. The horse was grey.*

*The figure in the background has a black hat with red and white plumes. He wears a polished steel cuirass and a buff coat. He has a red sash round his waist and red holster caps, all correct for a Private Gentleman of the King's Troop.*

# Fig 3: Horse Grenadier, Horse Guards, 1684

*The following details come from a description published by Nathan Brooks of the Review on Putney Heath by the King in 1684:*

*'The King's Own Troop, The Granadiers of this Troop have blew loops tufted with yellow upon red coats lined blew; with Granadier caps lined the same and a blew round mark on the outisde, armed with bayonets and harquebuzes.*

*'The Queen's Troop, The Granadiers clad and armed as the King's differenced by green loops with yellow tufts upon their coats.*

*'The Duke's Troop, The Granadiers, as the King's only distinguished by the coat loops of yellow upon their breasts.'*

*It would seem from this description that the only difference was in the lace loops on the coats, the facing colour being the same for all. Note the early form of Grenadier (or Granadier) cap. Later this type of cap became more stylised and took on the more familiar mitre shape. See also colour plate on page 17, which shows detail differences, though only one year later.*

# Fig 4: Trooper, 2nd Troop, Horse Guards, 1712

*This shows the uniform of the Horse Guards in 1712. The detail is taken from a painting in Marlborough House. The tricorne is black felt bound in gold lace, and the hair is natural colour tied with ribbon. The scarlet coat has blue cuffs and lining with all lace gold. The carbine belt has two blue stripes set in gold lace. The pocket slashes are laced gold and all buttons are gilt. The waistcoat and breeches are in dark blue cloth with gilt buttons. The belt buckles are brass. Black knee boots are worn. The cloak shows the blue lining uppermost and the scarlet edges shows at the sides. The pistol housings are blue, laced gold with a blue stripe. There appears to be no Crown and Cypher on the housings. The horse furniture is black with brass buckles.*

# Fig 5: Officer, 4th Troop of Horse Guards, c. 1740

*This is taken from a portrait of Captain James Miller, who served in the 4th Troop. It gives detail of an officer's uniform at this period. The head-dress is a black tricorne hat laced in gold with a vandyked pattern in the lace, a gold tie, and a button. The coat is of scarlet cloth, lined blue with blue cuffs and scarlet flaps laced in gold. The lace on the coat is all gold of a looped pattern with tasselled ends. The waistcoat is buff, gold laced. The sword hilt is gilt; gloves are buff leather and the breeches would also be buff.*

# Fig 6: Trooper, 3rd Troop of Horse Guards, 1742

The 1742 'Cloathing Book', as it is usually called, had as its full title 'A Representation of the Cloathing of His Majesty's Household and all the forces upon the Establishments of Great Britain and Ireland'.

The work was compiled due to the Duke of Cumberland wishing to record the uniform of the Army.

The book depicts troopers of the four different Troops of Horse Guards, and though the same basic print is used for each figure the differences seem to be very carefully made. All have red coats with blue linings and cuffs, and what appears to be a small piece of blue material edged with gold lace buttoned at the neck (see the drawing here). All lace was gold; the waistcoats and breeches were of a light buff colour and do not appear to be laced. The white knee pieces were worn to protect the breeches from wear against the stiff knee-boot. Sword hilts were brass.

The differences between the Troops were the stripes on the carbine belts and colours of the housings: red for the 1st, white 2nd, yellow 3rd and blue 4th. The holster caps and housings all had the same design featuring gold lace edging and the Royal Cypher in red within the blue garter, all surmounted by a Crown. However, the colour of the ground cloth followed the Troop colour. The lace on the housings appear as if fringed in 'Cloathing Book' illustrations.

The cloaks were red, lined blue. At this period the hair was powdered and tied at the back.

# Figs 7 & 8: Private Gentlemen, 1st Troop, Horse Guards, c. 1750

Fig 7

In the 1750 period the Horse Guards consisted of two Troops (the 3rd and 4th Troops were reduced in 1746), to each of which were attached a Troop of Horse Grenadier Guards. When the 3rd and 4th (Scots Troop) of Horse Guards were disbanded 20 Private Gentlemen from each were transferred to the 1st and 2nd Troops of Horse Guards.

The illustrations show the uniform worn at this period. The tricorne hat was black bound in gold lace, with a gold cord tie and button. Coat was scarlet with blue lining. Collar tabs, cuffs and turnbacks were all laced in gold. The carbine belt was laced in gold with two crimson stripes. Buff waistcoat and breeches, white knee pieces, and black jacked boots completed the dress. The housings

*Fig 8*

are of red cloth, bound in gold lace with light red between. The Royal Cypher is
on a red patch. It incorporates a blue garter with gold lettering and edging and
crown in natural colours. The cloak was rolled with blue lining to the outside.
All harness was in black leather with brass buckles.

Fig 8 is after a contemporary oil-painting by Parrocel in the Royal Collection.
It shows a trooper of the 1st Troop. This painting shows clearly the lace on the
coat as being in single loops and having the skirts laced in gold. Monier, on
the other hand, shows a trooper of the 1st Troop with lace in pairs and a
scarlet edging to the skirts. The reader must make up his own mind which is
correct, but there is a strong possibility that one of these originals was wrongly
recorded at the time.

The 2nd Troop of Horse Guards were different in having two blue stripes on
the carbine belts and blue housings. Otherwise the uniform followed the
above description, the lace on the coats being in twos.

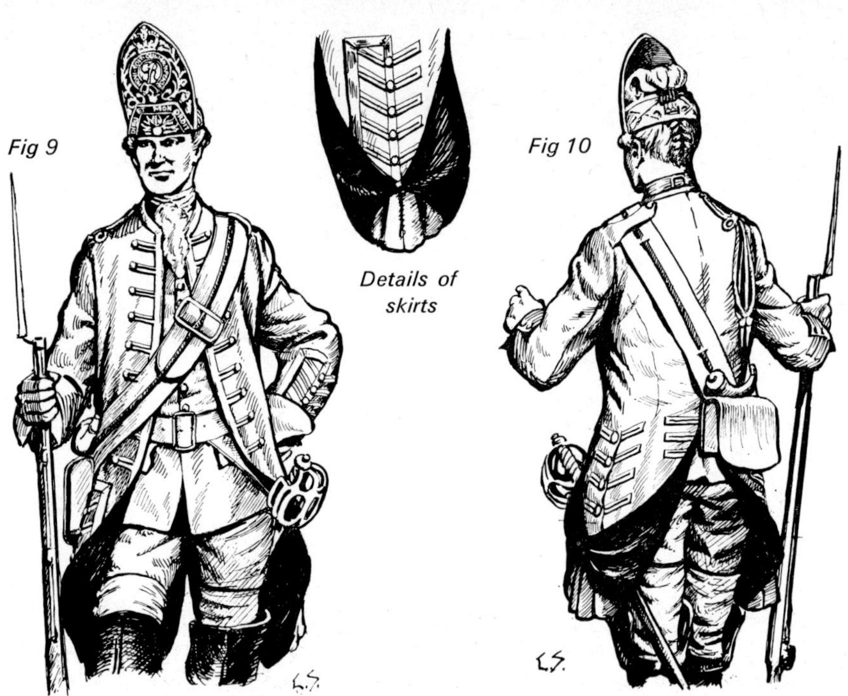



# Fig 9: Quartermaster,
# Fig 10: Private, 1st Troop,
# Horse Grenadier Guards, 1751

*The cap is blue fronted and embroidered with the Crown and Cypher within the garter and the scroll decoration is white; the little flap is red, edged with yellow, with a grenade and possibly the trophies behind it in white embroidery. The cap itself is of red cloth and the turn-up behind is also red and is embroidered with crossed sword and musket and a grenade in white. (Parrocel's painting depicts a back view of a Horse Grenadier showing this detail, but as Mr. Lawson says in his 'History of Uniform', the embroidery shows what appears to be crossed sword and musket and what looks like a drum on the back part. I think this may possibly be a grenade, though I have illustrated it as a drum in Fig 10.)*

*The coat is red lined blue, without lapels and laced possibly in this case as Quartermaster in silver. The blue cuffs are laced in silver with a broad silver lace round the edge of the pocket flap, on the skirts and cuff flap. This is evidently the rank badge of a Quartermaster (the rank of Quartermaster should not be confused with the modern counterpart in the Army; this rank then was not administrative, but similar to the modern Squadron Sergeant-Major). The waistcoat and breeches are buff and there are white knee pieces. The Quartermaster carried the same accoutrements as a ranker.*

*The dress of the Private (Fig 10) is the same as the Quartermaster except that all lace is white and he has no broad lace on the pocket and cuff slashes. The pouch belt for both carries a blue flask cord; all belts were buff. There was a steel hilt to the sword and a bayonet was carried in the buff waist-belt. The shoulder knot was white.*

**Plate 1: Horse Grenadiers, 1685:** *(Left to right) Grenadier, 1st Troop; Grenadier, 2nd Troop; Grenadier, 3rd Troop. Details based on Sandford's contemporary description of the Coronation of James II.*

# Fig 11: Private, 2nd or Scots Troop of Horse Grenadier Guards, 1751

*The 2nd Troop cap has the front of red cloth, edged white and has the Crown, Cypher and Garter as for the 1st Troop (see page 16), but the embroidery has the rose, thistle and foliage on either side. The little flap is blue, edged white with a large white thistle and having a yellow scroll with 'Nemo me impune lacessit' embroidered. The turn-up at the back is blue, edged white and has the crossed sword and musket. The back of the cap is red with a white tassel.*

*The coat is red, lined blue with blue cuffs. All lace is white and the shoulder strap is red. The flask cord is red. Waistcoat and breeches are buff and knee pieces white. Black boots were worn with steel spurs. The buff belts, gloves, sword, bayonet, and musket were as for the 1st Troop, already described.*

*The housings are red, edged yellow, with central stripe of blue, and a narrow outer edge of red. Normal coloured Crown and Cypher appeared within the garter.*

*The housings of the 1st Troop differ in being blue with a double yellow lace which had a red central stripe. The rest of the design is the same as the 2nd Troop. The cloaks in both cases were red and blue.*

# Figs 12 and 13: Trumpeter, Life Guards, c. 1750

*The 'State' coat of the trumpeters at this period has really remained almost unchanged and is still worn practically the same except for the hanging sleeves (for a later comparison see Fig 56).*

*The tricorne was black bound in gold lace with gold tassels and cord tie. The coat was of scarlet cloth with blue cuffs. This was very heavily laced in gold, having the Royal Cypher on back and breast. The trumpet was silver and the trumper banner featured the Royal Arms on a crimson ground embroidered in gold, silver, blue and red, with a gold fringe.*

*The sword belt and frog was laced in gold with two scarlet stripes, the buckle being brass. Sword hilt was also brass with black scabbard and brass mount. Black knee boots were worn with steel spurs.*

*Not visible in the line drawings is the buff waistcoat laced with gold. Buff breeches were worn with white knee pieces. The housings were of scarlet cloth laced with gold, and with the garter and Cypher below the Crown on holsters and saddle cloth. The cloak was blue with red lining. Harness was black leather. Trumpeters had grey horses. Many bandsmen at this period were negroes, recruited specially for band service.*

**Plate 2: Horse Guards, c. 1750:** *Troopers, 2nd Troop of Horse Guards (mounted) and Trooper, 1st Troop, Horse Grenadier Guards. Background (left) is a Trooper, 2nd (Scots) Troop of Horse Grenadier Guards.*

**Plate 3: Officers, 1st Life Guards, c. 1790:** *Shown wearing full dress. Troopers in background.*

# Fig 14:
# Sir Philip Ainslie, 2nd Troop, Horse Grenadier Guards, 1763

*This drawing is taken from the engraving by Scott of the portrait painted in 1763. The coat is of scarlet cloth lined with blue, blue collar cuffs and turn-backs, all the lace gold with gilt buttons. The waistcoat and breeches are of white Kerseymere, crimson sash. The cap appears to be the normal fur Grenadier cap, but the detail is not clear.*

*The sword hilt was gilt (in the portrait the sword and scabbard have been removed from the shoulder-belt frog). The scabbard is black leather with gilt mounts. Black knee boots complete the uniform.*

# Fig 15: Trooper, Horse Guards, 2nd Troop c. 1767

The illustration is from a series of paintings of the Guards at Darmstadt. It details the change of the uniform from the 1751 period. The head-dress remained similar, still tricorne with gold lace binding. The hair was powdered and tied with a queue, and there was no pigtail as previously. The coat was scarlet and lapelled now with blue, with gold lace set 2 by 2. The low collar is bound with gold lace. The blue cuffs have gold lace set in two, and the pocket slashes have a similar arrangement of lace. The blue turn-backs were laced all round in gold. Unseen in the illustration would be two bars of gold lace in the middle of the back at the waist. The carbine belt seems to be very similar to the 1751 pattern, having two blue stripes with gold lace and a steel spring clip. The sword appears to have been of the old type. Breeches and waistcoat were white. The housings were blue with gold lace with blue line, with the usual garter, Crown and Cypher on a red patch. The holster caps were of white fur and the cloak showed blue with red lining.

**Plate 4: Life Guards, 1815:** *Officer and Corporal (Sergeant) in service dress. Troopers in background. Rank of Corporal was changed to Corporal of Horse from 1878 when the new army rank of Corporal was introduced to the Household Cavalry.*

**Plate 5: Officers, c. 1821:** *Officers, 2nd Life Guards (left) and 1st Life Guards. Troopers of the two regiments are shown in the background.*

# Fig 16: Officer, 2nd Troop of Horse Guards, c. 1779

*The uniform shown is from a portrait of Major John Tempest, c. 1779. The hat does not appear to have embroidery but the coat is well shown; this is of scarlet cloth with dark blue collar, cuffs, lapels and epaulette straps. The loops are in gold lace and all buttons are shown in gilt. The white turnbacks shoulder belt appears to have a plate but is not detailed. The waistcoat and breeches were white with all buttons gilt, and a crimson silk sash. Black knee boots were worn. The sword hilt was gilt, and there were also gilt mounts on the black scabbard.*

# Fig 17: Trooper, Horse Grenadier Guards, c. 1780

From an uncoloured contemporary print the following details are noted:
usual Grenadier cap in black fur, white metal plate with Royal Arms; coat
scarlet without lapels, but with blue collar and cuffs; turnbacks white; all lace
plain white with white metal buttons; worsted fringed epaulettes; waistcoat
and breeches white; pouch belt and waist belt whitened leather. The pouch
appears to have the Coat of Arms tooled in the leather.

The housings were blue with yellow lace with possibly a blue line between.
There was the usual coloured Crown and Cypher within the garter. The sword
had a steel hilt. Pistols were carried in the holsters. The musket was carried
slung. The cloak was red with blue lining.

**Plate 6: 1st Life Guards, c. 1860:** *Officer and Veterinary Officer in full dress.*
*In the background, Trooper in guard order and Corporal (Sergeant) in full dress.*

**Plate 7: Field Day, 1887:** *Troopers, 2nd Life Guards in field day order. Infantrymen look on.*

# Fig 18: Officer, 1st Troop, Horse Guards, c. 1780

*The illustration gives another example of the pattern of lace worn by Officers at this period. The coat was scarlet with blue collar and lapels, the epaulette had gold embroidery on blue cloth with a gold fringe. The detail is based on a portrait of Peter Ryres Hawke. All lace loops are gold, the gilt buttons having a garter star decoration. The belt plate, just visible, has a blue enamel and gilt centre design. The rim is silver with a gilt design similar to the design of the lace loops. The waistcoat is buff with gilt buttons.*

# Fig 19: Officer, 2nd Troop, Horse Grenadiers, c. 1787

*The head-dress was black fur with a gold lace tassel and a gilt plate with the Royal Arms. The coat in this case was plain scarlet with scarlet lapels, only the collar and cuffs being blue with gold lace. The buttons are gilt and appear to bear the Crown over the Royal Cypher. The belt plate is a large silver star with a gilt and enamel centre and a Crown above. The white waistcoat was double-breasted with gilt buttons and a crimson sash round the waist. The epaulettes were of gold embroidery with gold lace fringes. The sword had a gilt hilt with an ivory grip, and there were gilt mounts to the scabbard which was of black leather. The details in this drawing are taken from a portrait of Lieutenant-Colonel Walton, 2nd Troop, Horse Grenadiers.*

**Plate 8: 2nd Life Guards, c. 1907:** *(Left to right) Trooper in church parade order, Corporal of Horse in undress order, Corporal in riding school order, Trooper in mounted drill order, Corporal in barrack guard order, and Trooper in walking out order.*

# Fig 20: Troopers, Horse Grenadier Guards, c. 1787

*Troopers at this period are shown and the detail is from a contemporary print of a Review at Blackheath in 1787. The Grenadier cap had a white metal plate of the Royal Arms and was of black fur. A white worsted tassel hung on the right side. The hair is powdered and plaited, turned up under the cap in the fashion of Grenadiers. The coat was scarlet with white lace loops, having no lapels. The collar was blue and so were the cuffs. All buttons were white metal. The fringed epaulettes were white worsted. The coat was lined white, while the pouch belt and pouch were of whitened leather. The sword was suspended from a waist belt with a brass buckle. Waistcoat and breeches were white and knee boots black.*

# Fig 21: Officer, 1st Life Guards c. 1796

The head-dress was black felt, laced around in gold lace and the plume was white over red feathers. The coat was scarlet with a scarlet collar, the lapels and cuffs being dark blue. The gold lace was in pairs of square-ended loops on the lapels. The epaulette was of gold lace and fringed. Turnbacks of the coat were in white cloth, with gold on the blue skirt ornament. Waistcoat and breeches were white; all buttons were gilt. The crimson sash was worn over the coat and tied on the right side. The belt plate was oval gilt with the Crown and Cypher and rim in silver.

The holster caps and shabraque were of scarlet cloth, bound in gold lace with a scarlet centre stripe. The Crown was embroidered in gold and the star in silver.

# Fig 22: Officer,
# 2nd Life Guards, c.1796

*The dress of the 2nd Life Guards differed in the arrangement of the gold lace on the lapels. The loops were large, equally spaced, and very close together. The epaulette and cuffs were also different, and the turnbacks of the coat do not appear to have been edged with gold lace. The head-dress was similar to the 1st Life Guards but in the 2nd the plume was black. The belt plate was rectangular with cut corners and a Crown and Cypher all in gilt. The sword hilt was gilt with gilt mounts.*

*The rest of the dress is the same as described opposite for the 1st Life Guards.*

# Fig 23: Officers, 2nd Life Guards, c. 1802

The two figures depicted in the illustration are from contemporary drawings by Robert Dighton Jnr. The head-dress of the figure in the back view is the full dress gold-laced bicorne, while the other figure has his bound in black. Both have the plume held in gilt scales with a black cockade. Large gold tassels are shown on each hat.

The back view figure has the full dress coatee with gold-laced collar, which was of scarlet cloth. The skirts had gold lace loops with gilt buttons. The turn-backs were white edged with gold lace, the skirt ornament being gold wire on dark blue cloth. The equipment was in white leather with a black pouch and Coat of Arms ornament in gilt metal. The sash was crimson silk. White breeches and knee boots complete the dress.

The facing figure wears the frock uniform which was scarlet with blue collar and cuffs. The double-breasted coat had gilt buttons. The cuffs and skirts were ornamented with gold lace loops. The rest is similar to the above description. Dighton shows this figure with a rectangular belt-plate, which was said to be used only by the 1st Life Guards, the 2nd having an oval one.

# Fig 24: Troopers, 1st Troop of Life Guards, c. 1805

The figure showing a back view has the bicorne laced with gold, a white over red feather plume and gold tassels. The full dress coat has a scarlet collar, laced all round in narrow gold lace, gold epaulettes, gold lace loops on cuffs and skirts, white turnbacks edged gold, and small gold lacings on dark blue skirt ornaments. White gauntlets, hide dark blue cuffs. All equipment was of whitened leather. The black pouch had brass ornaments. Sword knot was white on the heavy cavalry sword of 1796 pattern. White breeches were worn with knee boots. The hair was powdered and tied with a black ribbon in a pigtail.

The front view figure is the same, but he shows the blue plastron style coat front heavily laced with gold loops. Both men are shown armed with a musket and bayonet. The details are taken from a water-colour painting by Atkinson, c. 1805.

# Fig 25: Officer, 2nd Regiment of Life Guards (Full Dress), c. 1812

*The detail on this drawing is taken from one of a series of prints published by Colnagi and engraved by Stadler from drawings by Charles Hamilton Smith on the 'Costume of the British Empire' c. 1812–15. It shows the full dress of the Regiment prior to the adoption of the coatee and helmet. Colours were as follows:*

**Head-dress:** *Black; bound in gold lace and tie; Garter star badge in gilt; gold tassels.*

**Coat:** *Scarlet, with scarlet collar, blue cuffs and lapels (cuffs not seen, but would be blue); all lace gold; gilt buttons; black stock, white skirt frill, gold aigulette; white turnbacks edged with gold lace; gold on blue skirt fastening; crimson sash tied in the rear.*

**Equipment:** *White belts, black pouch with gilt ornament. Breeches white; black knee boots; sword knot white leather with gold tassel.*

**Horse Furniture:** *Scarlet shabraque; all lace gold with blue centre stripe; gold embroidered Crown and silver Garter star. Black saddle with holster caps in black fur; white head stall and lead rein.*

# Fig 26: Officer, 2nd Life Guards in new appointments c. 1813

*A Warrant of March 12, 1812, directed that a helmet with horse-hair crest was to be adopted. A print by Goddard shows the 2nd Life Guards in 1814 with the type of helmet as drawn, and an actual helmet is in the Household Cavalry Museum. Engraved on the front plate is '2nd LIFE GUARDS'. This helmet was replaced by the black and red crested helmet with all-brass peak (for Officers), as in Fig 28.*

*A scarlet coatee with blue facings was adopted at the same time as the helmet was taken into wear and the illustration gives a good impression of the uniform circa 1813. In 1814 sabretaches were taken into wear and the scarlet shabraques disappeared. In their place was adopted sheepskin shabraques and blue horse furniture. The blue and yellow sashes of the men were changed to scarlet and yellow.*

# Fig 27: Troopers of the Life Guards in service dress, 1815

*This was the dress of troopers during the Waterloo campaign. The head-dress was black with brass ornaments. The crest was black over red with black again underneath. The peak was black with brass rim.*

*The coatee was scarlet with blue collar patches and cuffs (not shown in the illustration). The lace on the collar, epaulette straps and cuffs was gold. The material of this coatee was rather coarse. The girdle was yellow with scarlet stripes. All buttons, buckles and badges were brass. Normal issue included haversacks and water-bottles. Grey overalls with broad scarlet stripe down outer seams were worn on campaign. The sabretache was black leather with brass garter star ornament. All belts were of whitened leather, the black pouch had brass ornaments and the sword was steel with a steel scabbard.*

# Fig 28: Officer, 2nd Life Guards, c. 1815

This illustration is based on a picture by Sauerweid of Brevet Lieutenant-Colonel R. Fitzgerald, who was killed at Waterloo. The uniform appears to be the full-dress coatee with gold lace over the collar and down the front. The girdle is scarlet and gold. Pouch belt was white. Grey overalls were worn. Blue horse furniture was gold laced, and a black sheepskin was worn with the saddle. The head-dress is as described before with an all-brass peak. The sabretache would be all black with gilt ornaments (Garter star).

There is another print of an Officer of the Life Guards wearing his Waterloo Medal and dressed similarly, except for the coatee. In this case he wears the single-breasted button type as for service, white breeches and knee boots, and an undress sabretache as described above.

# Fig 29: Trumpeter, Life Guards, 1816

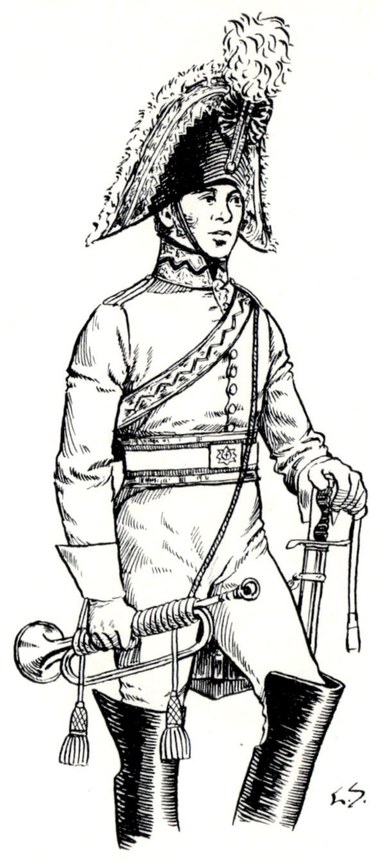

Sauerweid depicted a trumpeter of the Life Guards among his many drawings of British troops after Waterloo and the line drawing is based on this representation of the uniform. The lace on the figure was all gold and the zig-zag line through the lace on the collar was blue; the pouch belt had gold lace with a blue line edging; the girdle is striped crimson, which colour just shows each side of the white sword belt. The single-breasted coatee was scarlet with blue facings. White breeches and knee boots complete a most striking uniform.

The head-dress was the bicorne ornamented with broad vandyked gold lace. The cockade was black, secured by a gold loop and button. It was lined with scarlet feathers and the plume was of white feathers.

The trumpet was silver with gold and crimson lines. Sauerweid, also in this series of drawings, depicts a kettledrummer of the Life Guards whose dress is very similar to the trumpeter, except of course for the trumpet and sword belt, sword and slings. The pouch belt in this case has a blue zig-zag line in the centre.

# Figs 30 and 31:
# Pouches and Sabretaches

*Fig 30*

*Fig 31*

**Fig 30: 1st Life Guards, c. 1814**: *This was the full-dress pouch and sabretache taken into wear in 1814. After Waterloo it was altered slightly, in having two scrolls added 'Peninsular' and 'Waterloo' as shown in a subsequent illustration, c. 1817 (Fig 32). The embroidery on both was of gold lace and gold wire and sequins on a dark blue velvet ground. The Garter Star is set on a trophy of arms in coloured sequins and gold and silver wire. The Crown above had a crimson cap.*

**Fig 31: 2nd Life Guards, c. 1820**: *This illustration is copied direct from a pouch and sabretache in the possession of the Parker Gallery and Captain Hollies-Smith is of the opinion that it was worn about 1820. The lace is gold and the design is in gold wire, the two labels reading 'Peninsular' and 'Waterloo' (on the sabretache the honour 'Waterloo' is on the right of the grenade, and 'Peninsular' on the left, opposite sides in fact to that on the pouch). The whole is on a blue velvet ground.*

# Fig 32: Officers,
# 1st Life Guards, c. 1817

*Both Officers are shown in full dress, but one is drawn in overall trousers, which were worn at times. The head-dress is the 1817 pattern ordered by the Prince Regent; it was polished steel with brass ornaments and black bearskin crest.*

*The coatee was scarlet cloth with all-blue collar and cuffs all laced gold. White gauntlets were worn. The turnbacks on the tunic were blue. The cuirass was of polished steel with gilt ornaments. Pouch belt was blue, edged in gold lace. The cuirass lining was blue cloth. Sword belts, etc, were all gold on blue leather with gilt buckles. The sabretache was in design similar to the drawing on page 43, but now had the battle honours 'Peninsular' and 'Waterloo' added above and below respectively. The sword was of Household Cavalry pattern with a heavy gold sword knot and tassel. The pouch was also similiar to the one shown in Fig 30, except for the two honours now added. The overalls were of a claret colour with gold lace. The right-hand figure has white breeches and knee boots.*

*Dighton does not show epaulettes or aiguillettes, neither does E. Hull in his coloured print of an Officer, 1817.*

# Fig 33: Officer, 1st Life Guards, 1817

*This shows the Evening or Ball Dress of the Officer of the Life Guards. The coatee is double-breasted, of scarlet cloth with blue collar and cuffs, and the tails have no turnbacks but are tailored to shape; all buttons were gilt, all lace gold. Epaulettes and aiguillettes were gold. Head-dress was a cocked hat with gold ornaments and white feather plume. Dress sword was gilt with ivory grip, gold knot and gilt mounts to scabbard. White cloth breeches and silk stockings were worn with black buckled shoes. Details for this uniform are based on a Dighton water-colour painting.*

# Fig 34: Officer,
# 2nd Life Guards, c. 1820

*Full dress is shown. The head-dress is as described in Fig 35. The coatee was scarlet with blue collar, cuffs and turnbacks, all lace in gold, with gilt buttons. The epaulettes were heavy gold bullion and aiguillettes were gold. The cuirass was polished steel with gilt ornaments. The pouch belt was gold lace (oak-leaf pattern) with dark blue edging. The pouch and sabretache would be similar to the one described in Fig 31. The overalls were claret colour with gold lace stripe (oak-leaf pattern) on the outside seam. The black sheepskin had scarlet vandyking, and the shabraque was dark blue with gold lace edged in scarlet, and a gold grenade ornament.*

*The Officers' chargers at this time were either black, bay, brown, or chestnut (Brigade order—May 13, 1814) and in one case an Officer had a grey.*

*The 1st Life Guards shabraque differed in shape from the 2nd. It was square-ended instead of round, and the ornament was the Garter Star instead of the grenade. Detail for this drawing is taken from a water-colour by William Heath.*

# Fig 35: Head-dress of the Life Guards, c. 1822

*In about 1825 the ornamental brass plate on the front of the cuirass disappeared and the cuirass was then practically as it is today.*

*The head-dress is described in detail in the 1822 Dress Regulations: 'Grenadier bearskin about 20 inches deep, a large gilt plate at the bottom, with gilt raised King's Arms and regimental badge; a gold bullion tassel at the top, from which proceeds a gold plaited cord line passing over the left side of the cap behind, looping at the bottom and continuing across the front of the cap and fastened on the right side with a rich flounder and bullion tassel suspending, gilt engraved scalet, a large gold embroidered grenade behind, a small gilt socket at the bottom on the left and added to all this was a white feather "about three-fourths of a yard long".'*

*Later a helmet was also worn, a crested version with a steel body.*

# Fig 36: Helmet, 1817-1832

*This helmet was introduced in 1817. It was of a polished steel, the ornamentation being gilt. The plate on the front had a Hanoverian Coat of Arms with the battle honours 'Peninsular' and 'Waterloo'. The troops had a similar helmet of a slightly different shape, being lower and squatter. The ornamentation was similar but in brass. Both had the bearskin crest.*

*In full dress the bearskin cap was worn.*

# Fig 37: Officer, 2nd Life Guards, c. 1822

The detail of the illustration is taken from a portrait of Captain Alexander McInnes, which was featured in an article by Major A. McAnnand in the 'Journal of the Society of Army Historical Research'.

The helmet is the crested 'Roman' type, although the Dress Regulations, 1822, state the head-dress was the bearskin cap. As we know, however, the 'Roman' type was worn at times as well. The helmet was of polished steel, with a black bearskin crest; a brass rim to the peak and a gilt-rayed plate. The plate design was the Coat of Arms with the battle honours 'Peninsular' and 'Waterloo'. Head and chin scales were of gilt.

The coat was of scarlet cloth with blue velvet facings, the collar and cuffs being embroidered in gold lace. The aiguillettes and epaulettes were in gold. The pouch belt and sword belt and slings were all gold lace of oak-leaf pattern, edged with blue. The waist strap of the cuirass was also of this pattern.

The cuirass was of bright polished steel with brass studs and lined with blue velvet. The cuirass scales on the shoulder were brass. The sword is shown in a brass scabbard and hilt, the ornamental plate has the crest of England beneath the large Crown. The sword knot was white leather with a gold and crimson tassel.

Dress Regulations state that a girdle of crimson and gold lace would be worn.

The breeches were white, as also were the gauntlets. On the pouch belt the Waterloo Medal is shown.

# Fig 38: Farrier, 2nd Life Guards, c. 1825

In the possession of Parker Gallery was a contemporary oil-painting of Farrier P. Simpson, 2nd Life Guards, from which the detail above is taken. The bearskin cap with scarlet feathers is well shown. The chin scales were brass. The coatee was dark blue with gold-laced collar. The epaulettes had brass crescents and scales. On the painting the buttons on the single-breasted tunic are rather small. White leather equipment was worn, with the waist-plate in brass. The design is indistinct. The axe has a short ornamental handle in wood and brass. The axe-head cover was black. The gold farrier badge was on the right arm. White gauntlet gloves and white breeches were worn with black knee boots. The horse furniture was black, the saddle brown leather, and the shabraque was in black lambskin.

# Fig 39:
# 1st Life Guards,
# 1830

**Farrier** *(foreground)*

The farrier is in the dress worn c. 1830. His head-dress is of bearskin and has a brass plate and chin scales, and the peak is partly covered by the fur but the edge of the peak is bound in brass. His coatee is of dark blue cloth with a scarlet collar which has gold lace on each side of the front in a ribbed pattern. The cuffs are blue, edged with narrow gold lace. The buttons were brass, as were the shoulder scales. The equipment is of white leather and the belt-plate is brass. The farrier's apron is white and appears to be fringed. The axe is carried in a white leather shoulder belt and the axe-head cover is black leather. The wooden shaft had a brass mounting. Overalls were claret colour with a scarlet stripe. Sword was of normal pattern steel with white leather sword knot. The gauntlets were white leather.

**Officer, Undress Frock** *(left)*

The black shako-type forage cap had no ornaments. The blue frock coat had gilt buttons and gold cord shoulder straps. Overalls were claret with a scarlet stripe. A white pouch belt, black pouch, dress sword with gold sword knot, a black scabbard with gilt mounts, and steel spurs, completed the dress.

**Trooper, Barrack Guard Order** *(right)*

Forage cap was claret colour with a scarlet band. Coatee was scarlet with blue cuffs and collar was gold laced. Brass scaled epaulettes, brass buttons, white gauntlets, and white pouch belt, were worn. He carried a carbine but wore no sword. Overalls were claret with a scarlet stripe.

# Fig 40: Corporal, stable dress, Corporal-Major, walking out dress, Trooper on fatigue, 1st Life Guards c. 1828

*This shows different undress orders. The Corporal in stable order wears the forage cap of a brownish-claret colour with a gold band. His shell jacket was of scarlet cloth and had plain blue collar and cuffs, and nine gilt buttons down the front. Three gold chevrons and a Crown were worn on his right arm. (Regimental) Corporal-Majors wore a Crown above a four-bar chevron on their right arm in shell jacket. The dress is completed with white trousers and black shoes.*

*The Corporal-Major wears his gold aiguillettes from his left shoulder and has brass shoulder scales. (Only chevrons and Crowns were worn on the 'undress' jacket.) His coatee of scarlet cloth has the blue collar laced in gold, the blue cuffs being also laced in gold. He wears a gold laced girdle. The overalls are of a claret colour with a broad scarlet stripe down the outside seams. Black boots and steel spurs complete the dress. His forage cap is the same as the Corporal's described before.*

*The trooper in the background on fatigue wears the forage cap with a scarlet band, and is in shirt-sleeve order and wearing the white trousers and black shoes. He wears a white shirt.*

# Fig 41: Troopers, 1st Life Guards, full dress, 1829

*The dress of the troopers at this time was very ornate and must have been a very colourful sight to the spectator at parades and guard mounting. The bearskin cap was worn in full dress and was the same as described for Fig 35. The coatee was of scarlet cloth laced in gold, the collar, cuffs and turnbacks dark blue. Small brass grenades were used as skirt ornaments. The brass shoulder scales had dark blue cloth lining. The cuirass was of plain polished steel, the brass star ornament having disappeared about 1825. All the fittings were brass. The waist retaining strap was of whitened leather with a brass buckle. The cuirass lining was dark blue cloth.*

*The pouch belt was white leather with black polished pouch and brass ornament, and steel carbine swivel. Sword belt was worn under the cuirass, but over the coatee, and was white with white sword slings. The pouch belt now had the 'flask cord' which was adopted by the Life Guards in this year (Brigade Order, June 27, 1829). In this case the colour was red, the 2nd Life Guards having blue. White leather gauntlets, white breeches, and black knee boots completed the dress. Sabretaches and the Officers' sashes were laid aside also in the year 1829.*

*The crested helmet was worn for guards and duties (GSO, November 19, 1821) and the carbine was usually carried on guard duties.*

# Fig 42: Trumpeter, 1st Life Guards, c. 1833

*This shows the dress of a trumpeter and the detail is from a contemporary oil-painting by Dubois Drahonet. The head-dress is the steel helmet with brass-rayed plate, but in this case the crest is red, the rest of the ornaments being the same as the other ranks.*

*The coatee was scarlet with blue facings. The lace was a special pattern, gold with blue vandyked light on the collar. On the cuffs the gold lace was vandyked. The cuirass was polished steel with blue lining. There was a white cuirass retaining belt and a pouch belt with red 'flask' cord. The mountings were brass on the cuirass. The overalls were blue with scarlet stripes. The trumpet banner was crimson, with the Royal Arms in full colour, gold ornamentation and fringes. There were flying cherubs over the top of the Royal Arms.*

*A general order of August 2, 1830, abolished moustaches in the Cavalry except in the Life Guards, Royal Horse Guards and the Hussars.*

# Fig 43: Trooper, 1st Life Guards, c. 1833

The 1831 Dress Regulations confirm the Life Guards as still having the 'Roman' helmet with black bearskin crest, but the bearskin cap was still worn in full dress. In 1833 King William IV introduced a new Grenadier cap and plume in place of the 1821 pattern. It was lighter and had less ornamentation than that shown in Fig 35. It was described in the 1834 Dress Regulations as being 14 inches deep in front with gold bullion tassels on the right side and a gilt grenade. A long plume of white swan's feathers was on the left side and went over the top. Gilt leaf scales were attached to lions' heads roses.

The coatee was single-breasted with brass buttons and scarlet with blue collar, cuffs and turnbacks. On each skirt was a grenade and brass scale epaulettes. The cuirass was as described for Fig 41. White leather breeches and black jacked boots completed the dress. Undress trousers were at first a distinctive brown or claret mixture, with scarlet stripes down the outside seams, but by 1833 the Life Guards had dark blue trousers with scarlet stripes.

The sword was the Life Guards trooper pattern of 1829. The carbine still appears to be the old flint-lock pattern. Detail comes from Dubois Drahonet paintings, Windsor Castle.

# Fig 44: Corporal, 1st Life Guards, c. 1833

The dress of the Corporal follows the general appearance of the trooper in *Fig 43*, except that he wears aiguillettes on the left shoulder in gold cord and the figure is shown in overalls of claret, soon to be changed to blue cloth with a broad scarlet stripe down the outside seams. The rank of Corporal in 1833 was equivalent to the rank of Corporal of Horse (Sergeant) today and the aiguillette had no knots above the tags. The Regimental Corporal-Major wore epaulettes and his aiguillette had a knot above each tag.

The sword had a steel hilt with brass studs and a white sword knot. The sword belt was worn under the cuirass and had white sword slings. The cuirass had a brass edging and studs.

# Fig 45: Trooper, 2nd Life Guards, c. 1833

*This detail is from a picture attributed to 'Alken' which shows the uniform of a trooper at this period. In general the dress agrees with the painting by Drahonet of the trooper of the 1st Life Guards, only in this case the flask cord is blue and the shabraque is blue with gold embroidered grenade and number '2'. The wide gold lace is edged with scarlet; there was a white lamb's wool saddle cover; all harness was black leather.*

# Fig 46:
# Officer, 2nd Life Guards, c. 1833

*The 'Roman' helmet was worn for most duties except full-dress parades, when the bearskin cap was of course worn. The pattern was as described in preceding pages. The coatee was, of course, scarlet with blue collar, cuffs, and turnbacks; buttons were gilt. Gold lace embroidery was carried on collar and cuffs, and an embroidered grenade on each of the skirts. The cuirass was of bright polished steel with gilt mounts and studs, and had dark blue lining or 'Pickadels'. The pouch belt was in gold lace with the blue flash or flask cord. There were gold cord aiguillettes and the cuirass retaining strap was gold lace. The sword belt was worn under the cuirass and had sword slings of gold lace with blue edges. The sword hilt of Life Guards pattern was gilt and there was a steel scabbard. The sword knot strap was of white leather with gold and crimson tassel. Steel spurs would be worn. Waist sash was in gold lace.*

*In the 1834 Dress Regulations the sword for the 2nd Life Guards is described as having three scrolled and chased bars, and the steel ornamented on both sides with a large brass grenade. However, according to Dubois Drahonet the hilt appears to be of the same design as that of 1821.*

# Fig 47: Trooper,
# 1st Life Guards, c. 1849

*The illustration is of a trooper in the dress just prior to the Crimean War. The new 'Albert' helmet was of polished steel with brass ornaments and chin chain, and was introduced about 1842. The Garter Star was in white metal and the plume holder was of a leaf pattern. Plume was white. There was scroll work on the peak (this is shown in a print of a Corporal dated 1849 by Alfred De Dreux, on which the illustration is based. In the De Dreux print a Corporal is depicted, but he wears no aiguillette, only two gold stripes and a Crown, possibly an omission by the artist). The trooper has a gold laced collar; the coatee is scarlet with short tails and blue turnbacks. White gauntlets hide the blue cuffs and gold lace. The steel cuirass is similar in pattern to the previous description. Pouch belt was white with red flask cord. A small black percussion cap pouch is on the right side of the white waist retaining cuirass strap. White breeches and black jacked boots were worn. White sheepskin edged with blue was worn with the saddle and the harness was black. A 1842 pattern percussion carbine is carried.*

# Fig 48: Officer, 2nd Life Guards, in Frock uniform, c. 1849

*The uniform shown is taken from a painting believed to be by Henry Barrand, as described by Major A. McAnnand in an article in the 'Journal of Army Historical Research'.*

*The head-dress is the black oilskin forage cap. The frock-coat is of blue cloth with scarlet collar and lapels. The double-breasted coat is fastened by gilt buttons. The epaulettes are of blue cloth bound with gold lace with gilt crescents. Within the crescent in gold embroidery is '2 LG'. A gilt button is placed at the collar end of the epaulettes, with a gold lace fastening. The pouch belt is of white leather with a blue flask cord, a black pouch, and gilt ornaments. The white leather sword belt is fastened by an oblong belt-plate featuring a Garter Star, over which is a Crown. On each side is a cypher 'LG'. The sword had a brass hilt; the scabbard was steel and the sword knot white with gold tassel. The blue overalls had two broad scarlet stripes with a $\frac{1}{2}$-inch blue line between in the centre of which is a $\frac{1}{4}$-inch narrow scarlet piping.*

# Fig 49: Trooper, Life Guards, (Camel Corps), 1884-5

*In 1884 the Life Guards took part in the Nile Expedition. They were mounted on camels and the dress at this time is shown here. The head-dress was the foreign service white helmet with white puggaree. The equipment was a brown leather bandolier with '1882 Improved Valise Pattern' pouch and belt— white haversack and water-bottle. The breeches were yellow cord with dark blue puttees. Brown boots and (possibly) canvas gaiters were worn. Their arms were the Martini-Henry Rifle Mk III of 1879 and bayonet.*

# Fig 50: Barrack Guard
# 2nd Life Guards, c. 1890

*The trumpeter on the right of the guard is as described for the musician in Fig 52. The Corporal of Horse wears the 2nd class aiguillette from the gold cord shoulder strap. His tunic is as for the other ranks—scarlet, blue collar and cuffs, gold lace on the collar and cuffs, a loop of gold lace with a button at the rear on the collar, and a loop in the shape of a chevron, with a button in the centre on the cuff. The edge of the tunic and skirt was piped in blue cloth. On the skirts at the back were two three-pointed flaps edged round three sides with similar piping. On the middle and lower points was a button. At the waist above the flaps, just below the sword belt, were two more buttons. All buttons were brass.*

*The troopers and Corporal wear the same tunic (there was no appreciable difference in the dress of a Corporal and Corporal of Horse in full dress). The troopers' shoulder strap was blue, edged all round with gold lace, fastened by brass button.*

*All ranks wear the steel polished helmet with brass ornaments and chin chain. The equipment is whitened buff leather. The pouch belt has the blue flask cord. All carry carbines and wear blue overalls with the 2nd Life Guards double scarlet stripe with scarlet line between.*

*From left to right the picture shows the Trumpeter, Corporal of Horse, four Troopers and a Corporal.*

# Fig 51: Staff Corporal Farrier, 1st Life Guards, c. 1890

*The forage cap is blue with a scarlet band, each side of which is a narrow strip of gold lace—gold tracing lace round the crown, gold embroidered crown on the front, and black patent leather chin strap.*

*Tunic was blue with scarlet collar and cuffs. The collar, in addition to the gold loop and button, had the gold lace run round the top as well. The cuffs had the chevron loop and button, but the upper and rear edges of the cuff were also laced in gold. The gold embroidered Crown and horse-shoe was worn above the cuff on the lower right arm. There was a gold 2nd class aiguilette. All buttons were brass. The pouch belt and sword belt was as for other ranks, having, of course, the red flask cord and the single stripe on the blue overalls. Sword was steel with black grip and steel scabbard.*

# Fig 52:
# Bandsman and Band Corporal, 2nd Life Guards, c. 1890

*The musicians wore a distinctive tunic, as shown here. It was of scarlet cloth with blue collar and cuffs which were edged all round in gold lace. Along the inner edge of this was a line of 'bullet holes' in gold braid. The bandsman had a distinctive type of shoulder strap in gold lace. The tunic was edged all round, down the front, round the skirts and skirt flaps in gold braid. There were no buttons on the skirt flaps or cuffs. The Band Corporal wore the 1st class aiguillette with a gold corded shoulder strap. All buttons were brass. The plume was red for the band and trumpeters. The sword belt, slings, overalls and helmet were as the rest of the dress of the other ranks. Pouch belt had a blue flask cord. The pouch was black with brass ornament.*

*Trumpet-Majors were dressed as for the Band Corporal but had, in addition, the distinction of a Crown and crossed trumpets in gold embroidery on the lower right arm above the cuff.*

*Musicians at this period did not have buttons on the skirts of the tunic.*

# Fig 53: Officers' undress frock, 1st and 2nd Life Guards, c. 1900

**Forage Cap**: *Blue cloth, with scarlet cloth band, and scarlet welt round the crown; gold embroidered peak of regimental pattern. The 2nd Life Guards had a gold French braid figure on the top.*

**Frock-coat**: *Blue cloth, single-breasted, the collar ornamented with figured black braiding, and figured black braiding on both sleeves extending to 12 inches from the bottom of the cuff. Six loops of $\frac{3}{4}$-inch black braid down the front on each side, with two olivets on each loop, $\frac{3}{4}$-inch braid on the outer seams of the sleeves and back seams, with eyes and fringe at the waist and tassels on back skirts. Shoulder straps edged with $\frac{1}{2}$-inch black mohair braid, fastened by black netted button.*

**Overalls**: *Blue cloth, with scarlet cloth stripes of regimental pattern down the outside seams: 1st Life Guards had two stripes welted $1\frac{1}{2}$ inches wide; 2nd Life Guards $1\frac{1}{4}$ inches wide and $\frac{1}{2}$ inch apart, with a scarlet welt between the stripes.*

# Figs 54-55: Corporal, 1st Life Guards— Corporal Major, 2nd Life Guards c. 1893

*The photograph of a Corporal of the 1st Regiment, compared with that of the Corporal-Major of the 2nd (next page), shows that outwardly, to distinguish the difference in rank was impossible. Both wear the 2nd class aiguillette and the corded epaulettes were to all appearances the same. The regimental distinctions were very small. The collar of the 1st was squared, where the 2nd was slightly rounded. The flask cord, of course, for the 1st was red and for the 2nd blue. There were other very minor differences quite indistinguishable to the layman. The colours of the general uniform were: Head-dress polished steel, brass mounts, silver Garter Star, brass chin chain. Tunic scarlet cloth, blue collar and cuffs, all lace gold. On the collar a loop of gold lace with a button at the rear end on each side of the collar, and a hollow chevron with a button in the centre on each cuff. The edge of the tunic down the front and the skirt was piped with blue cloth, and on the skirts at the back there were two three-pointed flaps edged round three sides with similar piping. On the middle and lower points of each there was a button, and on the waist, above the flaps, two more buttons. The sword belt was placed just above these. The cuirass was of polished steel with brass orna- ments; 2nd Class aiguillette was in*

gold lace with gold cord epaulettes.  There were white leather gauntlet gloves, buckskin breeches and jacked boots with steel spurs. Pouch was black with brass ornament Garter Star and Crown with reversed cypher and labels.

# Fig 56: Trooper and Trumpet Major, 2nd Life Guards, c. 1893

*The trooper follows the general description of the details of the Corporal and Corporal-Major, except for the aiguillette.*

*The Trumpet-Major is in State dress with the blue 'jockey' cap and the scarlet and gold laced frock-coat. The Royal Cypher was carried both on breast and back. The description of this dress is similar to that described for Figs 12–13, except for some minor differences such as the collar shape and hanging sleeves. The trumpet banner also is similar down through the years except, of course, for the changes in the Royal Arms.*

*The uniform on the amalgamation of the 1st and 2nd Life Guards, as mentioned in the Introduction to this book, went through many minor changes until finally, about 1928, the dress was more or less as it is today. The red pouch belt cord of the 1st Life Guards was taken into wear throughout, (the 2nd Life Guards had previously had blue). The lacing of the tunic was carried out to 1st Life Guards pattern and the 2nd Life Guards overalls were adopted. An entirely new button was devised and a new pattern for Officers' shabraques.*

A Barrack Guard sentry at his post in bad weather. The forage cap is dark blue with a red band. This man is from the 2nd Life Guards in 1882.